The J Horoscope

THE J HOROSCOPE

POEMS

Sharon Chmielarz

2 0 1 9

Also by Sharon Chmielarz

Different Arrangements
But I Won't Go Out in a Boat
Stranger in Her House
The Other Mozart
The Rhubarb King
Calling
The Sky Is Great the Sky Is Blue
Love from the Yellowstone Trail
Visibility: Ten Miles, a Prairie Memoir in Photography and Poetry
The Widow's House
Little Eternities

Copyright © 2019 by Sharon Chmielarz
All rights reserved.
Printed in the United States of America

Brighthorse Books
13202 North River Drive
Omaha, NE 68112

ISBN: 978-1-944467-17-3

Cover art: *Genesis*, 2007
6" x 4", gouache, palladium leaf on paper
by Nancy L. Purington
Copyright © 2007 by Nancy L. Purington
www.nancypurington.com

Author photo: Mark Cryderman

Brighthorse Books is a small publisher of poetry, short fiction, and novels based in Omaha, Nebraska. For information about Brighthorse Books, visit us on the web at brighthorsebooks.com. For information about the Brighthorse Book Awards, go to https://brighthorsebooks.submittable.com/submit.

Brighthorse books are distributed to the trade through Ingram Book Group and its distribution partners. For more information, go to https://ipage.ingramcontent.com/ipage/li001.jsp.

To the Ancient Story Collectors

Contents

Note to the Reader   1

INTERSECTION #1	3
Yahweh the Stork *re* the Family	5
A Basket of Apples	6
INTERSECTION #2	7
Abe	9
The Boatman's Wife	10
Yahweh the Stork *re* the Storyteller	11
The Cuckold's Dream	12
A Lot like Lot's Wife	13
Luck Out for a Walk	14
Oh, Daddy, Daddy, Daddy Lot	15
One Interior Life	16
INTERSECTION #3	17
Yahweh the Accountant	19
The Animals	20
Dove with Hint of Green Backs	21
INTERSECTION #4	23
The Foxes	25
Lost in Love	26
INTERSECTION #5	27
To Joseph the Dreamer, the Pretty Boy	29
Joseph the Dreamer's Wife	36
INTERSECTION # 6	37
These Earthlings May Have Seen Yahweh	39
Miss Yahweh in P.S. #1	41
The Dream Maker	42
Yahweh the Stork *re* "He Had It Coming"	43
INTERSECTION #7	45
The Gardener in Eden	47

INTERSECTION #8	49
Eve's Daughter Marilyn	51
Cain	52
Yahweh the Stork *re* Mother One Heart	53
The First Old Woman to Have an Egg Planted Between Her Legs	54
The Seven Days of Postpartum	55
The Family Album	56
Yahweh the Cook	57
Trailers for *Life Is Good*	58
INTERSECTION #9 61	
Re the Tree of Life, a Dialogue	63
Yahweh the Avenger 64	
Flies, Theology 1. & Flies, Theology 2	65
INTERSECTION #10	67
Yahweh the Rock	69
A Play of Few Lines, In the Underground	70
Yahweh the Stork *re* Estate Sales	72
INTERSECTION #11	73
Where One Becomes Two	75
Yahweh the Stork *re* the Tree on Highway 1	76
INTERSECTION #12	77
Yahweh the Stork *re* A Human Condition	79
INTERSECTION #13	81
The Host	83
Notes on Individual Poems	85
Acknowledgments	89

Note to the Reader

Look. A woman is writing on parchment, a scroll.*
We don't know her name. Her king, Solomon, has
died, and the whole country's going to hell under the
new king, Rehoboam. The year is 937 BCE. Banished
from the ring of political power, she grounds herself
by collecting the kingdom's ancient stories. Of the
four writers in *Genesis*, J is the one who delivers
the earthly creatures—Noah, Joseph, Jacob, Rachel,
et al—and, to paraphrase Pogo, they is us. Her cast
of characters includes the god Yahweh (or Jahweh)
who can appear in various guises. She's named J for
her intense interest in Yahweh's character.

---

*The Book of J, David Rosenberg and Harold Bloom, 1990.

"Now look: man becomes a creature of flesh."
#1, p. 61, *The Book of J*

INTERSECTION #1

*Mango. The color surprised us, flew
over us in the eye of a bird, in feathers.
We couldn't get enough of it.*

*Not salmon, not tangerine. Mango.
It turned our teeth pink.
Each laugh was a bite of it.*

*We left hatred behind for mango.
Even blame, which we couldn't
let go of*

*quite, even our blame
drummed mango,
mango to our ears.*

*We danced to mango
close like lovers. Mango's
sweetness melted us into life.*

YAHWEH THE STORK *RE* THE FAMILY

I've seen it all—the father who killed his son,
the sons who threw their brother down a well,
the father-in-law who ordered his son's wife
burned to ash, it's happened under orange roofs
on this very street where nary a wind stops.
From the town's light pole, my nesting place,
I watch a kid on the curb, kicking stones,
yearning for something more, like new relatives,
though if they arrive, park their blue car
at the front gate, tumble out, helloing, spilling
their stories and habits all over the living room,
they'll truss the kid up with their family ties.
The next day I deliver another baby, a bundle
of trust; yes, babies have to trust, that's the first
unspoken contract with the world. The first forgotten.

A BASKET OF APPLES

Take a basket of apples
 along for the road and horse blankets
  from the barn. But don't
   belly back here for more.

No forgiveness, no tool
 to erase each little
  shitty minute from
   the universe's giant

mood swings. On their own
 they nuzzled out names:
  From Cassandra, Cassiopeia,
   Itasha, Ekaterina evolved

Eve of the Possible. Possibly
 from Alfredo, Alvie, Alois,
  Albert, Al or Marvin sprang
   Adam His-Bushelbaskets-Full.

Condemned to dust
 they gave their bodies
  to battles, a war they
   signed up for, skirmishes—

Who's on top? Who's under?
 Under the love we say
  we do live, we
   do, the wind whispered.

Theirs were amorous shadows
 running through woods,
  pre-Daphne and Apollo.
   No one mistook them for deer.

INTERSECTION #2

*There she was. She'd bought an apple red
BMW and drove it with gusto. Crash!
She didn't see Him coming. Well, it was His fault,
too. They both jumped out, waving their arms.*

*He, with louder vocal cords, was the first
to drive away. She stood on the corner,
waiting, fuming; hours passed like eons.
Her whole day, her life, damn it, ruined.*

ABE

Then came the Abrahams, the Abrams, the Abes,
the Arthur Millers and Saul Bellows, Yahweh's
salesmen whom Yahweh promised seed as countless
as the sands on the shores of Lake Michigan.
The men with the *go* throbbing in their groins,
a gift from Yahweh. *And if there's one thing we are,
it's we never give up hawking our pyramid schemes.*

O, yes, they made a few heads turn on their way
from parking meter to office door to secretary, a doll
at a desk. They usually got their order in if you know
what I mean. Hey! Doesn't every man want to know
a Thursday night woman? Remember? *Go ye therefore
and populate the earth?* Or something like that.

The little woman's home keeping supper warm,
the kid happy, wriggling his toes in his crib. Daddy's
driving home at night through little prairie towns
en route to Chicago and singing, *Daddy loves you,
oh, my, how Daddy loves you, You're Daddy's
one and only little boy.*—A pretty nice voice, his mother
used to think. A nice little baritone, she always said.

THE BOATMAN'S WIFE

She spent mornings on the ark corralling
the stupid hens. Not one head whacked
off for dinner.
                In the aviary
birds shivered watching her search
nests they had with difficulty hidden.

She wished she could shit like a bird
before taking off and fly straight out
of this whole mess.
                In storms,
bailing out the boat or hunting down
loose snakes, she longed for books

left on the shelf at home: Joseph Campbell,
James George Frazer.
                Thinkers! Unlike
the Boatman, who believed every damned
rain drop was prophecy,
                throwing his head back,
gulping rain down, letting his beard grow
long and ratty.
                He numbered the days
in charcoal marks on the walls,
and evenings fashioned tiny Eves

from rib bones.
                She never
should've married him. Penned in
for the rest of her houseboat life.

How long would that last?
At least she could save the birds.

At least, this one dove—

YAHWEH THE STORK *RE* THE STORYTELLER

I can't say who started it, but HE, the immigrant
and a hunk, the Boss's best worker, left her room
running, his leather jacket flung over a chair, his
cherry coke and new car-musk odor clinging
to air. And SHE, the Boss's Wife, who'd asked
if he'd 'attend her,' stood in a muddle of white
A-line robe with white boa collar, a perfect
nest for her chin when she winked. She the
Vamp, parading around her bed. She the Lover
in a sea-green negligée, undoing her hair. He
swallowed hard and made eyes for the door.
I won't say the flirtation meant nothing,
but surely a Mae West moment turned sour.
She may have hoped he'd steal back to her room—
he did not. Her maid heard the Affronted One's
yowl, came running, saw the new leather jacket.
Hubby the Boss saw the Victim, her messed-up
hair. *Who done it?*—She kept her mouth shut.
And sure enough, the plot evolved on its own.

THE CUCKOLD'S DREAM

You see the power of a dream, one dream
that explains why pain and the devil exist
in this lopsided paradise. You see how one
dream cradles crow and sacrifice. You see
in a dream's proselytizing how manna's
image hardens into generations of bread.

I listen to the why, the good that makes
what is mysterious about us, which is
a story's direction, leading from one thing,
plunging back at will to cover complications,
like the pure, fragrant joy found in eating
with your woman. I forget everything for flavor.

A LOT LIKE LOT'S WIFE

If he had an ace, would he win? If he had a king?
If he had the Queen of Hearts, would she go to bed
with him? If he had a deuce, he'd be set for life.
Luck, be my lady tonight.

He put everything he owned on number 7
and lost. Even the house. What to say to the wife?
She'd never leave. She loved the place.
The yellow kitchen. The peonies out back.

The homey hollyhocks along the fence.
The garden bower where she sat afternoons
with her feet up. Let him deal with it. But here's
the joker: one way or other, she was staying.

LUCK OUT FOR A WALK

Maybe a long afternoon. Maybe rain the challenge.
It pops an umbrella up for the underpopulation.

Maybe a place to hide. In a crowd Garbo
never wanted her face seen either,
too many people stopping, wanting favors.

Luck's own round world. Stylish black. The handle,
a shepherd's crook turned crook-curve down.

She loves rain's thrum on satin. Old fashioned.
Socially acceptable like an arm to hold onto.
Maybe her man catches up.

Ducks under.
Until the downpour lifts then—

OH, DADDY, DADDY, DADDY LOT

We didn't look back, didn't stop running
until we reached the wild mountains.
Treeless slopes, sooty and leprous-looking.

The vineyard Daddy planted struggled, parched.
His gray eyes, our gray eyes, not trusting
any straggler wanting shelter.

Left behind, down there in the valley,
Mom's salty body. The river reeked
of carcass. We three slipped into drinking,

making up games. My sister's
and my belly puffed up like melons.
Must have been the strange berries we ate,

we told Daddy. Show me the bush, he coaxed.
We hunted all night, up and down over shabby
slopes, up and down, up and down.

ONE INTERIOR LIFE

The name of their life could be loss,
a view taken at dusk, a shadow
standing at their door, a beast
with four legs in their room.
Like the bed in the mirror's
reflection.
                    A pool
of pallor slips over the floor,
ices the walls; theirs, too small
or too large, wrong side in.

The corset on the floor, too great
or insignificant to be stepped over.

Admit the interior had nothing before
they paid for the use of the room.

INTERSECTION #3

out in the field
saddened
sons of heaven came down

began the fond calling
wild animals
dove

forty days, forty nights
at the door
I will erase

a statue
looking back
on mythic fame

YAHWEH THE ACCOUNTANT

He rose in the accounting department
the way a homemade boat rises and rolls
over waves of maxed-out plastic and overdrafts.

Mr. Cool. His clients, prime for a geographical cure.
They polish the last martini off over the sink,
toss the gin bottle into recycle, creating

an avalanche of clinking dead soldiers.
No longer theirs, this repossessed house
hosts a list of defects the Accountant checks off—

It's better to sell at a loss. He offers oars.
He counts forty days into nights.
He cuts their boat's ropes to the shore. He waves

goodbye to Mr. and Mrs., their kids, dogs and cat,
gerbil and ferret, parakeets and snakes. The wife
waves back with her copy of *Wuthering Heights*.

THE ANIMALS

They crossed the waters in a long house,
shaped like a slipper with a barn door.
A seaworthy vessel, if you've never seen
a sea. Its only criterion was balsam's: to stay
afloat on Yahweh's darkest breath.

The animals were a patient lot. Sheep
grazed not far from the lion. Tigers frolicked
but not enough to frighten llamas or giraffes.
And a pair of black and white steeds,
delicate as dancers, led the oxen up the plank.

They were the great noise they would've made
had the waters rolled over them. They were
a moving territory, those elephants, big rump
rhinos, and a half moose-half bear ready to be
saved from the far shore's pale green fog

swallowing the cities Sodom & Gomorrah.
Rain had started; the lion's human face
was an aside to any future audience. *Is
this boondoggle or apocalypse?* Sooty
clouds warned of the fire to come.

DOVE WITH HINT OF GREEN BACKS

Toward evening as on Fridays
when the heart sings,
and the eagle flies,
a little note dangles
from the dove's beak.

Words in black ink
run with the magic
a bank can cash. *Dear bird,
I thrill, so
relieved to read of your nest.*

INTERSECTION #4

An olive twig, like stone on stone, prayed for.
Game sumptuous in his mouth, the man grows
prosperous, a dim blur blessed. He must remain.

A day will come, a vision to grasp, to overcome
in love, to groan with pleasure, groans
that spread into groans, as if with lightning.

What will you pay me to visit my homeland,
bring out gifts, a wife?
What will you pay her if she takes you in?

THE FOXES

And in the magic of that hour they turned into foxes
playing together undisturbed. Red foxes.

And when she was young, her hair glinted in sun.
And when he was old, she called him Silver Fox.

He thought she was the right girl for him.
At first she didn't like his accent. Too foxy.

But he bought things for her, gold bracelets,
bronze notions, wake-up calls, that sly fox.

His pulse jangled at the thought of her, beside
her, on her, in her, her *Dig deeper, Mr. Fox.*

Too late, her father's postings on his field's
borders: Beware of Guns & Dogs, Fox!

LOST IN LOVE

Once an owl flew into the tree's
other, leafy city. I was beyond you,
beside myself, barely breathing.

I didn't turn on a light, didn't move
from my shadow. I was wanting
the god calling outside the window,

the One Voice,
the lovely Who-who-
who circles the moon's horn.

INTERSECTION #5

In the grasp
he was in love.
(Run, don't look back.
Bring yourself out.)

Can you tell
everything
he tended, matured,
would appeal;
delivered,
burst its bounds?

He will follow
straight down to Sheol,
a garden,
rocked into the sea.

TO JOSEPH THE DREAMER, THE PRETTY BOY

You flee from your land to refuge.
This isn't what you planned, to live
as an exile drumming up work,
you, wild and lovely and common
as a broom. Girls like you. You are
tongue muscle from a foreign land,
a different language to be learned.
Your kiss falls lightly, at bee's speed.
Your smile is real not carved. Not like
a jack-o-lantern's botox grin.
In the land of the great far-flung,
the brilliance of your ways is sung.
And envy? Envy we now know
is madness. Be nimble, Joseph.

*

Be nimble. Be quick, dude. Jump—
                              They,
your jealous brothers, half-brothers,
will sell you. They threaten to wash
your suck-up mouth out with sheep shit.
They throw you down a well. You writhe
hours under the moon. Father howls
at the Sea of Crisis, *Come home!*
You never really wanted to
live in this world. Your mother would've
loved any child; she had you. You
came out the same place your dad slid
in. (Wonder! One that employs her
for the rest of her days.) She's your
door to this world under the moon.

    *

Doors to this world under the moon
open in dreams. What you can't grasp
by day is do-able in sleep.
Deep in the east, the mind does drama
drudge-work, like running for miles,
counting years of famine like cows,
finding the path from the bottom
of a well. Dream long enough and
someone's bound to come along, ears
itching for tales, tiny stages
morphing from lecterns to mountains,
rocks to lifts, stoves to bells to trees.
No one needs insight; dreams wrestle
for you. All you must do is see.

*

Yes, you! All you must do is see
your ten half-brothers, (not counting
your unnamed half-sister) stuck with
chores. It's not hard to figure out,
conceived as you were in the new
wife your dad is besotted with.
Because it never stops—*you* get
whatever *they* want most: a gift
from their father like the coat, pure
cashmere, bought for his favorite.
And when it's delivered, a box
seen from the older wife's measly,
chintzy window, it lands in your
arms. Of course they want to kill you.

*

Of course they want to kill you, you
own their very dreams, taking up
the whole bed as you slide in REM
time through dreams' glades, your heavy hand
gun loaded with retribution.
You blast away at will. Who's worse,
you ask the bears in dream parlance,
the hoodwinkers or the hoodwinked?
In the hush, X is the bully
you conquer. He/she/they bother
you no more. Your mind makes you free
and a rich man to boot. The path
to the past is strewn with spent shells—
you're out of there. You wake happy.

*

You wake happy. The wind has swung
from south to north. The harvest, in,
the winter wheat cut, shocked, and threshed.
The vulture drought by-passed your fields,
the refugee's, now landowner
of house and barns and granaries
bursting. Your brothers, thin, rain-starved,
ten hats on the hooks in your hall,
ten wagons, all begging for grain.
Thoughts storm in from all directions.
Memories tumble over slights.
Thunder shakes the grievances out.
The brothers gather on the porch,
you let them in to keep them dry.

*

You let them in to keep them dry,
men running into a promise
that may be a cage. You stay close
to the door and keep it unlocked
for speedy exits though strangely,
in the interim you've grown old.
While aiming at profits in rows
of years? Subtracting and adding?
You don't know. What's important now?
Your window breathes light and brilliant
use of shadow; some talk among
the oaks, not in words but in shade
and interval, like the dream where
you fled from your land to a home.

JOSEPH THE DREAMER'S WIFE

I'm the woman beside him who wakes
to cursing, tossing, moaning as he dreams
the future. He's the ex-pat in my country.

I'm the inheritor of white peacocks,
their elegant, useless, feathery strutting
in the yard. He loves them. Maybe

more than me. How can I work? I'm
the bitch who can't wait to be rid of 'em.
Their screech is driving me crazy.

I am the bee. The fragrance of the Dreamer's
skin lures me.—Let me kiss you, Love.
I offer almonds, pistachios, honey.

The day fills with dirty dishes and leftovers.
I'm the conniver. Tonight the loudest peacock
may suffer an unexpected accident.

INTERSECTION #6

*We were at the intersection
between Sodom and Gomorrah.
We were at the interstice of knowing
how far Yahweh would go, we were
testing him to see how fast he'd race
away from us, 0 to 60 in two seconds,
how soon he'd freak out at our worst,
even as we knew he'd let at least one
swallowtail escape, one transparent,
winged innocent elude damnation.
He'd give it time to flutter away
before he blew up the rest of us
sucked oranges, we who by nature
will do anything to fly high.*

THESE EARTHLINGS MAY HAVE SEEN YAHWEH

from the Babel Tower Gazette

1.

My purse was open on a chair,
an old man shambled toward me,
an old purse snatcher,
an old there's-fresh-fish-for-supper
smile on his face.
Was it him?

Small Fry

2.

I Hear That Lonesome Whistle,
                oo-ooo-oo.
Hey, Good Looking!
                I'm So Lonesome I Could Cry.
Why Don't You Love Me
                Like You Used to Do?
You were my thrill.

B. Hill

3.

Dam or damsel?

Puzzled

4.

He gives me three, small bells.
For my garden, he says, for my door,
and the table beside my bed.
Call me, he says.

Girl Next Door

5.

A red apple. Once perfect now
one cheek missing. The bite that hurt.

Ms. Snake

6.

So he wears a suit. So what? So does
the jeweler, hunched in his little, frayed shop.

FB Post

7.

How can a day already have passed?
I have done nothing, nothing.
Tsk. Pardon, my confusion.
It's only me, lounging in the sun.

Chrysanthemum

MISS YAHWEH IN P.S. #1

When they began that cloysome, fond calling—
Yahweh?—I didn't know them. It was fall,

I hadn't a seating chart or a lesson plan.
They'd soon smell it out, my lack of planning,

their noses keen as animals'. A dog's. A doe's.
I asked the blond boy in the window row

for his name, and the girl, very small for 7th grade,
in front of him. She dug inside her binder, laid

a notebook on her desk, pointed to a sentence in
a cosmos-sized story about names

that couldn't be hers. Just tell me what you want
to go by in school, I said. She actually panted.

How could this be so difficult? While I waited
for her name, the class tottered to their fate,

the wildness of the undisciplined and lost,
a frolic-y panic, an instinctive and natural chaos

in children, like a late summer storm in the yard
when all gains are lost in the apple yield.

THE DREAM MAKER

specializes in bean poles, snow banks, snappy endings,
sweeps wind aside in favor of quakes, rain, eclipse

    and fame's abyss,

sets time's own table with two plates, Late and Early,
arranges train whistles like pots above a stove

    on rails,

collects the day's remnants, crowds whose faces
can't be seen, developed from black & white photos

    of the dead,

loves your mind's open spaces, and you, defenseless
asleep in bed, a lot to work on, in the dark, drifting

    seas and oceans,

ranks the sandman's star higher than your own
on night's billboard, speckled with debris

    from broken glass,

pads about in slippers through your head, fastidious,
ingenious, servicing dreams' fragile business

    of speeding away,

pins down nothing but you, dead to a world
as unreachable as someone else's bells ringing

    in your ears.

YAHWEH THE STORK *RE* "HE HAD IT COMING"

Does that even make sense? *He had it coming?*
As if he's ordered something on line and waits
for a package to arrive by drone (or stork,
my deliveries centuries old). Nope, some hand-
rubbing unfriend is taking aim as casually
as an entrance or exit; in the door like a fly
and out like a head of state. I've flown
over plenty in war, impaled—stuck on pikes
along roads. Candidate-bullseye. Could be
you someday, plunked into your recliner, open
but guilty, then dumbstruck, indignant,
gobsmacked. I've learned when "it" is coming
via air or blood, punch or cyber, knock on
the door—the splat in *what?*—will hit the target.

INTERSECTION #7

*Job openings
were available
for guarding the garden,
listed in the international
registry of historic places.*

*Such a relief
the whole story
never happened. A relief
the scribe had simply found a job.*

THE GARDENER IN EDEN

He sat in a lawn chair while his neighbor
the scribe ghost-wrote his memoir.

This was in the days before birds and feathers.
Only wind and snakes were heard in trees.

Make it tart, Henry, the gardener mused.
Make the woman dangle from the story line.

Stories curled over their gray heads like pipe smoke,
a shroud dissipating into the garden's topiary.

*The female was a temptress. And remember
she obeyed a snake. Dissed me.*

It was autumn, the ground hardened with apples,
the deers' winter stock of apple fat.

Wasps searched gables and window sills.
The glade bee-loud, its roses tall as apple trees.

The gardener closed his eyes. *Make it sting, Henry.*
Henry sniggered. *And award her with curse.*

The rain that night was spotty, raising an odor
of dust and the gardener's tight lips. This was

in the days before the garden's overgrown paths,
when the gardener's roof tiles still held fast.

INTERSECTION #8

Looking for someone who'd like to be in a REAL NSA relationship. This is for real, let's talk and meet. You'll love my eager piercing eyes. I'm a man of the world. I love to kiss and deep subjects. Money's no problem. I like to do things rather than just talking about it, and there's a lot to do out here. I'm a little shy at first, but WOW, after I open up, I'm very fun to be with.

p.s. Only virgins need apply.

EVE'S DAUGHTER MARILYN

A piece of work—those bought and hung
in the gallery where SHE studied resemblances
between Picasso's jar and Roy Lichtenstein's,
Picasso's mistress and Jasper John's. She,
understanding an iota about the masters.

Face me. Look beautiful. Big smile now.
Let me see you without the blouse on.

Listen: She snubbed them. In that ravishing way
blonds have when a guard is watching. *Little*
jack horner sat in a corner . . . his mouth dropping
open . . . *eating his curds and whey* . . . , reaching
for his pocket (*he stuck in his thumb and pulled*
out a . . .) blackberry? (*What a good boy am I!*)

In dazzling spiked heels, she paused for full
effect over the floor vent, her white skirt
aswirl around two long, tanned lovelies.
All eyes in heaven bugged at her masterpiece.
It was the beginning of the world.

CAIN

We loved Harleys, the speed, the air in hair,
the gangs & gin & guns. On the road again.

And Mom? Laughing, *I've created a man,
just like God*. My bro and I were gods?
Or she was? She was funny that way.

Anyway, The Family Innocent got shot in a fight
with me over a girl. Not very respectable

when one son kills the other. And Adam-Dad?
Pretty defeated by then, always in danger
of apoplexy. *Go ahead*, he used to goad me,

bring more shame on our name.
Well, I tried my best, and I won.

YAHWEH THE STORK *RE* MOTHER ONE HEART

She's the tree the two hung from, suckling her plump,
ripe breasts, pushing their noses into her fleshy bags.
Mother of twins, she thanked me for the gift, raising
her hands, palms up—(Hear? The despairing sigh
among leaves?)—but is this what she'd prayed for?
One would've done, she said. And not the first born,
the rugged one his father loves, rather the second,
born to paint her portrait, his dark, sensitive eyes
flashing from the canvas to her pose: A tree,
a spreading tree, powerfully smelling sweet.
A tree with his initials heart-carved into the trunk.
A tree bent over the years from sheltering her
foxy son. As he speeds away in her lustrous black
Audi, she always waves, *Be home for supper, Love?*

THE FIRST OLD WOMAN TO HAVE AN EGG
PLANTED BETWEEN HER LEGS

Not that she didn't look at men, especially young men, the shirtless gardener, his nice, muscly chest, curvy brown shoulders, flat tummy caving down to the hairy place where the cock crows mornings, stirring and sweet. How old was she, having these seventh grade fantasies. He, her husband, had been up to all of them when they were young. You can't get pregnant from a wink though, which is about all she'd get from the gardener. She was old, for heaven's sake, groaning with arthritis; to be truthful, fearful: how would her bones hold up under the load of a man? But she had a dream and couldn't shake it. Why not make use of science? Didn't it promise a longer life? Cures? Babies? All the things she once prayed for. Clear skin, shiny hair. What you need today is money, a good doctor, a phone, and an insurance policy cheaper than a ten percent tithe. Who'd want a kid when she's sixty, some of her friends, grandmothers all, asked. Was it wise? When you're seventy, they'd clucked, the kid 'll only be ten! Wise-schmise. She wanted her dream lying red-faced and nibbling at her nipple. On the day the magic happened, for all the neighbors to see, she'd have a diaper run up the front yard's flag-pole, followed by her red, double-A bra. *You fly.*

THE SEVEN DAYS OF POSTPARTUM

I was so sore I hardly moved, why, they say, young women in labor have an easier time than the old.

I foresaw each day as two thousand years long. I set my course in maneuvering: If X happened, then I'd do Y; if Y, then Z.

Suckling my child, I saw the man in him. Fright shivered down my spine.

I bargained: Take my life, if ever need be, but spare my child's.

I ordered a feast, a goat, its head severed, the body roasted, proof of my steadfastness and humility.

From then on I lived ever after two-faced, keeping my thoughts to myself.

I wore an obedient demeanor, the way the jealous gods, the gods of death, like their women to dress.

THE FAMILY ALBUM

Over the years, so many days;
who can remember them all?

Walls bulge, windowsills swell
with the past. Children, popped

from the same, small pod, fly off
in different directions to work,

marriage; work, death. Goodness,
back into closed closets!

There's always the book, the drawer
that exists to be opened. And hands

of girls, comely, or only comely
in the dark, passed on in marriage

like the deed to the family cabin.
Think needlepoint. Think green

and blue stitching. On the wall,
framed, Old Aunt Tamar's saying:

*The first place he enters
is your arms. All your battles*

*take place on the bloody plain
between your two dusky legs.*

YAHWEH THE COOK

Had the man asked for the moon, his mother
would have found some way to pull it down,
all the while asking what else she could do.

Never would she send him so far away
as outer space, for how could she bear
her house if he were the night's cold face

smiling down on her?—I keep my hands
out of their intrigues. Are her woes
worth my while? Does she pay me for wits?

She pays me to cook. To keep the kitchen
orderly and the food smelling scrumptious.
Sometimes I joke. She frowns. Her son

nips at my ear. But things could be a lot
happier around here if she'd learn, as I have,
she can never fix the distance between them.

TRAILERS FOR *LIFE IS GOOD*

A woman looks in a mirror one morning and says,
"I guess I'm the one to make this family's name."
This said not with hubris, but a resigned willingness.

*

Don't the gods bless those who re-create their lives?
Well, he did and he was happy. Go, Lucky.

*

"That son-of-a-bitching brother of mine. And you helped
him, Ma. Git out of my way. It was MY money. I'm gonna
kill 'im."

*

Doing it vertical's nice if there's no choice,
but perpendicular's better, a roll straight
into the middle of gravity. And have I
mentioned the necessity of perseverance,
acquiring a financial umbrella?

*

The canyon was a cow shit sort of place,
deserted in fall when the kids go back to school.
Maybe I'm the only one in a tent guessing
there's a lot of wrestling going on at 3:00 A.M.,
like waking and thinking, what the hell is wrong with people?

*

Stall, stall was the Old Shit's middle name.

    *

Look at that moonlight falling through the window, making the window, like a man makes a woman. And their kids—they grow up so different. Shadowy.

INTERSECTION #9

All we've had since lightning struck is wind.
        Wind, wind, wind! Four days now.
Your chime
                in the back yard ash tree
        crashed, dashed.
                      I brought in the wash,
and it smelled
            all smoky.   *What the hell,*
                Yahweh?

RE THE TREE OF LIFE, A DIALOGUE

The tree was mighty. Rapturous.

    Grafted from multiple species.

I swooned under the spring blossoms.

    Snow snakes quickened along its branches.

A real eagle of a tree, right?

    A regular summer lounge: shade, breeze.

Since year Beginning and Ever Since.

    Yielding great fame and profit.

In fall the old tree bled apples.

    A major tourist attraction on Highway 1.

Don't ask us where it was. We swore . . .

    It's somewhere, but we've forgotten.

YAHWEH THE AVENGER

One day a girl prayed to me, *You know,*
this place used to be cool. Lots of parties.
Now I think you should nuke it.

Cities of light zapped into glitz and tinsel.
A man like Beethoven was lucky,
stuck in deafness, not catching the chaos.

Hear the violins' tremolo over the ruins?
My chilled angels. All things once loved—

the Rhenish pitcher, the Dürer rabbit—
sometimes I remember them with sadness.

FLIES, THEOLOGY 1.

Gawd, how
the flyswatter
hates flies.

FLIES, THEOLOGY 2.

Gawd, how
a flyswatter
loves a fat
fly.

INTERSECTION #10

That is the One.
The only One,
the One and Only,
a rock to every cipher.
Go figure!
little ciphers say.
Figure it out,
big ciphers say.

Who can hear
over their loud
numbering?
Out in the street now
they huddle, cheering
fabulous zero,
building on null.

YAHWEH THE ROCK

They never loved me. They never even liked me.
People prayed for a rock, and I was it.
And then I wasn't because they wanted me
to be like them: move, shout, scream,
show some spasm of expression. A rock?
What they missed, once they were alone
in a house in the desert, in a cabin or bankrupt
on a mountain, what they missed was a rock's
steadfastness, made of mineral, made of earth.
Humans waver, un-rock-like. No heft and girth
but pleasing palms. I like to lie in their shallows.
And I like to fly like a brick hurled against a tank
or skip swallow-like across a lake, or roll
clattering down scree into a guileless place.
A couple finds me. "This one's lucky," they say.
"Let's keep it forever." Frankly, very few do.

A PLAY OF FEW LINES: IN THE UNDERGROUND

Setting: the Underground Garage
Cast: Yahweh the Underground Garage Attendant;
    a Man; his Wife
Wife's Lines: *No space left for me* and *Drogi*,
    (a Polish endearment)
Yahweh's Line: *Lady!*

Yahweh appears from a cubby hole of an office
in semi-darkness behind a row of cars.
He-Who-Arranged-a-Space-for-Her
where she can park her car
turns his west face to her,

waves his arms, calling,
Lady!

She of Little Faith can't see him and continues to drive
in circles sniffling,

No space left for me.

Lady!

She the Blind One keeps searching
  for the garage's elevator—for that is
where her husband, her *drogi*, will come down to her.
How many times can she circle
park> park> park> park> park> ?

No space left for me.

Drogi will come down to her through the box-
carriage's sliding doors, and they
will drive away together out of the abyss.

An arrow pointing down lights up.
A rush of air in the shaft, doors shuffle open.
He's arrived. An old man

Drogi!

looking scruffy in a tan cashmere coat,
looking baffled and deaf.
The where-am-I-now look.

Lady!

Drogi!

Calls coil through the concrete
tunnels—

Drogi!
Laaaaady!
Drogi!

YAHWEH THE STORK *RE* ESTATE SALES

You can knock forever on a dead man's door—
Come on, get on up, you evil spirits—but the house
is properly cold and shut down. All the furniture,
divorced from the rooms. The ice box stands by
the lilac bush. Table and chairs, under the boxelder,
vow to stay together. In the garden the auctioneer's
flatbeds tout rows of mishmash, a half century's worth
of spare buttons and old-man shoes their owner hated.
Supper tonight's on the neighbors. Sugar-crusted
pies and salads dripping oil, noodle hot dishes,
buttered rolls, sticky blackberry jam for homesick tongues.
The front yard's fence gate hangs ajar (he'd have fixed it);
the hedge, leafless. His sons and daughters leave the sale
like strangers piling into a car and driving home.

INTERSECTION #11

Now look

death touches you

the tree I desired

you not to eat

settled there

dust you are

the snake

the woman

your man's body

eager above you

in labor

in labor

a deep sleep

a covering darkness

thrown over fear.

WHERE ONE BECOMES TWO

The old fox has died.
Now his mate is alone.
Now she must cross the river alone.

Look.
In the water.
Two foxes.

YAHWEH THE STORK *RE* THE TREE ON HIGHWAY 1

Never mind the black rot seeping through
its innards, its leaves' pallor suggested danger
moving in. How could the tree be nursed along
forever? Neighborly yellow-ribbon love,
huffs and lame denials, allied with the unfixable.
Sure they made a strong defense—the apple
blossoms' fragrance, rotund trunk, and *if*
it were cut down, who'd live so long to see
how tall a stand-in would grow. Tim the treeman
jumped from his truck shaking his head. The fact
was that *that* tree was a goner. Tim revved up
his chain saw. Sawed down, the tree landed in
flinches and fidgets, leafy swishes and a barren
thud. That's what still takes some getting used to.

INTERSECTION #12

How can terrible things happen you ask.
Only apple trees know.—Here, take a bite.
It's a honeycrisp. Like my mother used
to say about oatmeal for breakfast, Eat it.
It'll make you smart.

YAHWEH THE STORK *RE* A HUMAN CONDITION

Flying through time and topography to shelter,
I've heard it all from my nest on the stork pole.
A hundred-year-old woman conceives. A teen
gets pregnant but remains a virgin. Both have sons,
fuel for sacrifice. A knife blade through the chest
awaits one; torture, the other. The first saved
by a moment, the second nailed to a gallows
like a bloodied sack of millet. Stories! The night's
and a god's glut. Human kind swallows them
the way a hungry stork swallows a frog. In one tale
the gawky troupe of two servants, a boy and his
old man climb the mountain Jehovah-jireh.
In the second, the pregnant virgin rocks toward
Bethlehem on a donkey.—The Gauls and Saxons,
Greeks and Egyptians, Horites, Hyksos,
Swahilis and Anasazi, Tuaregs, Persians, Incas,
Anishinaabeg, and Mongolians make their own tales
from egg and sperm. That old Hebrew sheepman,
his face dripping with sweat, felt pressed into
offing his son. A knife aimed at the heart.
The moment on the mountain passed, and a voice
that sounded very much like his wife's rang out, "Enough!"

INTERSECTION #13

*Angels have fallen down the ladder
leading to and from heaven. Their wings,
broken, too crippled to do rungs.*

*Oh, their moth-like eyes. O, their hearts,
ground from blue diamonds. I hear their
Maker crying over His precious handwork.*

*Down on earth's luck now, this host.
All the stars in their heads shaken out.
Pray their robes turn into flying carpets.*

THE HOST

Like a farmer undone
    by bounty, bushed just thinking about the next
wheelbarrow load of radishes and zucchinis, she
        pins her mane
                back into a knot and calls for light.
Light for her table. The blue globe lamp emboldens
            platters of milky, husked corn, sheeny-green
peppers, the sausages' splatter—

    B r a t s b l u t a n d k n o c k w u r s t w e i s s w u r s t l e b e r w u r s t
    k i e l b a s a s a u c i s s e s a l c h i c h a s o s i j i p e m m i c a n—dozens

        of links and bags recorded in ledgers until
        the host covers her ears.

                Did you know

    the sausage maker begat the pastry maker;
    the hunter, the fisher; the gardener,
    the florist; the spice maker, the canner,

    all preservers, all of long lineage, smock-wearers,
praisers of oceans and lakes, amen, gardens and prairies,

yes! and the horizon's order of dawn and evening
        imprinted on the hungry, the thirsty,
                the between-meals.

Let's eat!
    A raconteur calls out. The raconteurs,
prone to thirst, arrive first, full of pomp and eager
        to earn their supper. For as the host says,

    a story's light around a table
(made of wood the violin maker suggested)

    or a light story is good.
As is laughter. As is ardor.

It is said, and much hoped to be true,
the host overlooked not one soul. Amen.

Notes on Individual Poems

PAGE 9 | "Abe"
   (God to Abraham:) "Bring yourself out of your birthplace . . . I will make of . . . your name, fame . . . ."—#30, p. 74 *The Book of J.*

PAGE 10 | "The Boatsman's Wife"
   "Yahweh shut him (Noah) in at the (ark's) door . . ."—#23, p. 70, *The Book of J.*

PAGE 11 | "Yahweh the Stork *re* the Storyteller"
   "She would appeal to Joseph day after day. . . . Recline with me."—#89, p.125, *The Book of J.*

   "Now look: as (Joseph's) lord hears his wife's words . . . his anger bursts its bounds. (He) took hold of (Joseph), threw him into prison . . ."—#89, p. 126, *The Book of J.*

PAGE 15 | "Oh, Daddy, Daddy, Daddy Lot"
   "Behind him, Lot's wife stopped to look back—and crystallized into a statue of salt."—#46, p. 87, *The Book of J.*

   "'Pity your lot—run, don't look back, don't stop until the end of the valley. Escape to the mountain or be crushed.'"—#45, p. 86, *The Book of J.*

   "But Lot went out from Smallah, toward the mountains, his two daughters with him . . . (and) settled in a cave alone with his daughters."—#47, p.88, *The Book of J.*

PAGE 17 | "Intersection #3"
   Each line is a segment from *The Book of J.*

PAGE 19 | "Yahweh the Accountant"
   ". . . the rain would be on the land, forty days, forty nights."—#23, p. 70, *The Book of J.*

PAGE 21 | "Dove with Hint of Green Backs"
"Toward evening (the dove) comes back . . . look: An olive twig dangles from its beak."—#24, p. 70, *The Book of J*.

PAGE 23 | "Intersection #4"
Also made of J-segments. The last line is a variation on "What will you pay me," (Tamar) said, "if I take you in?"—#84, p. 122, *The Book of J*.

PAGE 25 | "The Foxes"
". . . Rachel was finely formed, a vision to grasp . . . Jacob fell in love . . . "Jacob (was), . . . in the grasp of his love for (Rachel) . . . he entered . . . Rachel; he was in love with Rachel . . ."—#66 & 67, pp. 108, 109, *The Book of J*.

PAGE 27 | "Intersection #5"
Again, each line is made of segments from *The Book of J*.

PAGE 29 | "Joseph the Dreamer, the Pretty Boy"
"A many-colored coat was made for Joseph. His brothers grasped that it was him their father loved most; they hated him, could not speak warmly to him. . . . 'Look, here comes our master of dreams,' the brothers said among themselves. 'Now is a time to kill him, then throw him down an abandoned well.'"—#78 & 81, pp. 118–19, *The Book of J*.

He came out the same place his father went in is a quotation from *The Book of J*.

". . . Now look: he (Joseph) is in the house of his Egyptian lord. His lord could see that Yahweh attended Joseph, in whose hands everything that he tended, matured."—#88, p. 124, *The Book of J*.

PAGE 36 | "The Dreamer's Wife"
"They (Joseph's brothers) were served separately from him (Joseph), and from the Egyptians eating with him. They ate by themselves, because Egyptians could not bear to eat a meal with Hebrews (that would be an outrage in Egypt.)"—#99, p. 134, *The Book of J*

PAGE 47 | "The Gardener in Eden"
bee loud glade is borrowed from W. B. Yeats's "The Isle of Innisfree."

PAGE 53 | "Yahweh the Stork *re* Mother One Heart"
"Rebecca becomes pregnant. . . . When the twins are grown . . . Isaac loved Esau . . . but Rebecca loved Jacob."—#56. p. 96–97, *The Book of J.*

"Two nations," Yahweh said to her, "are inside you—two peoples already at odds in your belly."—#56, p. 97, *The Book of J*

PAGE 54 | "The First Old Woman to Have an Egg Planted Between her Legs"
"Within her, Serai's (Sarah's) side split: 'Now that I'm used to groaning, I'm to groan with pleasure? My lord is also shriveled."—#41, p. 82, *The Book of J.*

PAGE 56 | "The Family Album"
The first place he enters is your arms: "Entertain me," he (Judah) said, "in your arms. I wish to enter there."—#84, p. 122, *The Book of J.*

PAGE 58 | "Trailers for *Life Is Good*"
These are take-offs/out-takes based on Jacob and Esau stories. e.g., wrestling with the angel, stealing an inheritance, Jacob's courting. Rebecca was instrumental in Jacob's theft of Esau's legal inheritance.

PAGE 63 | "*Re* the Tree of Life, a Dialogue"
". . . Now Yahweh took (the earthling) out of the Garden of Eden, to toil—in the soil from which he was taken . . . settled there—east of Eden—the winged sphinxes and the waving sword, both sides flashing, . . . watch the way to the Tree of Life."—#10, p. 65, *The Book of J.*

PAGE 70 | "A Play of Few Lines . . ."
". . . You drove me from the face of the earth. . . . I return nowhere, homeless as the blowing wind."—#14, p. 67, *The Book of J.*

PAGE 72 | "Yahweh the Stork *re* Estate Sales"
"So Abrahm passed down all he had to Isaac. To his sons by concubines, (he) gave gifts, sent them away . . ."—#55, p. 96, *The Book of J.*

PAGE 73 | "Intersection #11"
Segments here also taken randomly from *The Book of J.*

Acknowledgments

The following poems, or previous versions of them, have been published:

The Cuckold's Dream: *Speakeasy*
Eve's Daughter Marilyn: *Kestrel*
Yahweh the Stork *re* the Family: *Louisiana Literature*
Intersections #2, 6, & 13 (as "Genesis," "Leviticus," "Deuteronomy"): *Commonweal*
The Boatman's Wife: *Cider Press Review*
These Earthlings May Have Seen Yahweh, section 5; The Seven Days of Postpartum; Miss Yahweh in P.S. #1: *Meditations on Divine Names,* and "The Host," Moonrise Press
Where One Becomes Two: *Lief* (online)
The Family Album: *Boomer Lit* (online)
The Animals: *Notre Dame Review*
One Interior Life: *Contemporary American Voices*
Yahweh the Avenger, Yahweh the Rock, Yahweh the Stork *re* A Human Condition, *The Hudson Review*

Grateful acknowledgment is given to the Collegeville Institute at St. John's University for providing me residencies. However, this book wouldn't have come into print without the help of editors, wonderful poets in "my" poetry groups, Norita Dittberner Jax's prompts re arrangement, and Jonis Agee and Brent Spencer, the publishers at Brighthorse Books. Long may they live!

SHARON CHMIELARZ was born and raised in Mobridge, South Dakota, three miles from the Missouri River. She graduated from the University of Minnesota and has since lived and worked in the Twin Cities. *The J Horoscope* is her twelfth book of poetry. Previous books have been finalists for the Independent Book Publishers Award, Midwest Book Awards, National Poetry Series, and the Next Generation Indie Book Awards. *Kirkus Reviews* named *The Widow's House* one of the 100 Best Books of 2016. *The Other Mozart*, a biography of Nannerl Mozart in poetry, was made into an opera. She is a recipient of *Water~Stone Review*'s Jane Kenyon Prize. Her work has been published most recently in *The Hudson Review*, *Burningword*, and *The American Journal of Poetry*. Her poems have been nominated several times for a Pushcart Prize (most recently in 2017, 2018, and 2019), and featured in "American Life in Poetry." Individual poems have been translated into French and Polish. The latter will be included in the 2019 anthology *Koncert w domu Szopena. Antologia poezji i prozy pisarzy polsko-amerykańskich*.

The Book of J was designed and set in type by Judy Gilats in Saint Paul, Minnesota. The text type is Maiola, designed by Veronika Burian and released in 2010. The display face is Adelle Sans, designed by José Scaglione and Veronika Burian and released in 2012.

www.ingramcontent.com/pod-product-compliance
Lightning Source LLC
Chambersburg PA
CBHW020144130526
44591CB00030B/217